What is my
DOG
thinking?

GWEN BAILEY

CHARTWELL
BOOKS

This edition published in 2016 by
CHARTWELL BOOKS
an imprint of Book Sales
a division of Quarto Publishing Group USA Inc.
142 West 36th Street, 4th Floor
New York, New York 10018, USA

ISBN-13: 978-0-7858-3431-1

Printed in China

First published in Great Britain in 2002 by Hamlyn,
a division of Octopus Publishing Group Ltd
Carmelite House, 50 Victoria Embankment
London EC4Y 0DZ
www.octopusbooks.co.uk

An Hachette UK Company
www.hachette.co.uk

Contents

Introduction

We would all like to be able to talk to our animals, to find out what they are thinking, ask them how they are, or find out why they do what they do. Sadly, we can't, and unless there is a breakthrough in scientific discovery or we learn to use telepathy, we are not going to be able to for the foreseeable future. So how, instead, can we find out what our dogs are really thinking?

If we study our pet dogs enough and watch what happens when they are in certain situations, we can build up a detailed picture of their body language, expressions and actions that helps us to guess how they might be feeling. Through my work as an animal behaviourist and through living with dogs all my life, I have been lucky enough to watch hundreds of dogs in different situations while knowing about their backgrounds and characters. I have seen how they appear to have similar emotions to us, and to react in similar ways. For example, they get depressed if they think no one loves them, they seem happy when a member of their family comes home, they get scared when threatened, and they enjoy playing games and having fun. If you add to this a knowledge of

the species differences between us and a detailed study of their behaviour, it becomes easy to guess what they might be thinking at any given time.

Acquiring enough knowledge to be able to do this takes time and is not so easy if you are new to the world of dogs or have not had time to study them fully. So this book is an attempt to help you to learn about what dogs are saying so that you too can begin to guess what they may be thinking.

There was a time when scientists considered dogs to be dumb animals, incapable of thought. Fortunately, this attitude is slowly changing, but we still do not have the scientific studies to back up the knowledge gained by experience. Perhaps we will one day but, until then, we have only our observations and experience from which to draw conclusions, which may or may not be right.

I have made an attempt not to be anthropomorphic and base my comments on what a human would think in the same situation. However, as a human, how I think will inevitably have an influence on how I empathize with others from a different species. Neither have I said what I think people may want to hear or what might be cute, but instead I have stated what I really think dogs would say if they had a voice.

I hope that you will find this book useful in helping you to work out what your dog and other dogs you meet may be thinking. By doing so, you will understand them better and hence give them a better life.

So frequently I see the results of misunderstanding between dogs and people. Dogs are blamed for all sorts of things they haven't done or weren't thinking because owners misread their body language, postures and actions. As humans with large brains and intelligence, it is our responsibility to learn about the language of the animals we keep as pets – I hope this book will help you to make a start.

Social animals

Wolves, the ancestors of our pet dogs, are social animals that enjoy each other's company. Humans have taken this trait and bred selectively over generations so the dogs we have in our homes are very sociable and loyal. Different breeds of dog will enjoy the company of people to different extents, but all like to live their lives in a pack with others, whether human or canine. Being with other members of the pack is important to them, and if they are denied social contact they can become very depressed or badly behaved.

More successful together

Wolves that live in a pack are more successful than those that live alone on the outskirts. They are safer in a group, more likely to kill large prey and so to be better fed, and are more likely to reproduce successfully. Being in a pack improves their chances of survival and those of the next generation and, therefore, a social existence is preferable to life alone.

You are my family

If puppies have become accustomed to being with people during the socialization phase, a sensitive period between weeks three to twelve of life, they readily accept the human family as their substitute pack. Similarly, human children readily accept dogs into their social world and both benefit from being together. Although dogs and humans have a similar need for companionship, we don't speak the same language and so communication between us is not always easy. Cuddling an animal you care about comes naturally to a human, but it is not something that dogs would do unless they were either fighting or mating.

DID YOU KNOW?

- Dogs have a similar social structure and internal drives to humans, which helps us understand their behaviour.
- Many owners mistakenly treat their dogs like children, although they are of course a completely different species.

We are a pack

Dogs readily accept others into their pack providing they are introduced carefully and there is no competition for scarce resources. Being with others gives security and companionship, which can be useful if affection from busy humans is in short supply. How well a dog gets on with others of his species is determined by how much time he spent with them in puppyhood. These West Highland white terriers grew up with other dogs and are more comfortable to be in close proximity than the collie, who grew up alone and is looking a little apprehensive.

Don't leave me

The need for social contact in our pet dogs is great and they prefer to be with their pack whenever they can. Some dogs are unable to cope with isolation and may panic when their owners leave. The resulting noise, destruction or mess in the house can be devastating for owners who cannot understand their dog's reaction. Dogs need to learn to accept being left alone from an early age if they are to cope well. Unfortunately, breeders and owners do not always appreciate this, and try to ensure that litter mates or people are with young puppies all the time so that they won't be lonely. Short, planned absences each day that are gradually extended as the puppy learns to cope helps them to learn to tolerate being alone, ensuring they can be left without problems when they are older.

I want to be with you

This dog is used to being hugged and cuddled by his owner and enjoys being with her. He trusts her completely and is totally relaxed even though he is in quite a vulnerable position. She is pack leader and is, therefore, responsible for keeping him safe and seeing off any threats. All the time he is with her, he can live a stress-free existence where his every need is catered for. Having her around makes him feel safe and he enjoys being close to her.

DID YOU KNOW?

- Dogs have a strong desire to be with others and if they are deprived of social contact they may run away or begin to exhibit attention-seeking behaviour to force their owners to respond.

Please come back

This dog would like to go too. Being left behind, even in the safety of his own home, is not good news. He can't know that the door is locked and a break-in is unlikely. Alone, he is vulnerable and could be attacked by anyone or anything that may decide to come in. Faced with this situation, many dogs try frantically to get to their owners by chewing at the doorframe or trying to dig underneath the door. They may bark or howl and many become quite panicky, resulting in a sudden need to go to the toilet leading to a mess on the floor. Some dogs have a view of the world as a safer place and aren't so worried about being attacked, but for others, only bad things lurk on the outside ready to come and get them.

I'll just spread these out a bit

Collecting together items that owners have touched or worn is a favourite behaviour for some insecure dogs when they are left alone. Surrounding themselves with a barrier of their owner's scent is a good way of letting others know that they had better stay away. Absorbent material such as tissue takes up the scent well as do television remote controls, which are often held by the owner and have little gaps around the buttons that collect dead skin cells. If these items are too small to form a barrier they are often chewed into pieces so that they can be spread out.

Saying hello

Most of us are familiar with the signals dogs use to greet us. The open-mouthed 'smiling' face and sweeping tail are well recognized and are signals for humans to approach and enjoy some friendly interaction. Different dogs greet people in different ways depending on how they have been handled as puppies. Some try to jump up to get to our faces, some enjoy being hugged, some want to be stroked and some just want us to acknowledge them and then play a game. Small dogs often want to be picked up and may dance noisily around our legs or jump against us until they are lifted up and cuddled. In all these different ways, dogs are signalling that they want the same thing – attention from us.

You're my friend

This dog knows this person well and loves to be with her. The dog would have been cuddled a lot when she was a puppy and now expects humans to cuddle her when they greet her. Her 'smiling' mouth, relaxed eyes and pinned-back ears signal her enjoyment. Her lolling tongue shows her excitement and her wagging tail indicates how pleased she is, although it curves under quite a lot which signals that she is not completely sure of her welcome.

It's too exciting

After the first greeting, she stands up, turns and leans her back end on the person. Dogs often do this when the situation becomes too intense and they wish to put some distance between their head and the person. In this position she can be stroked along her back and she will feel more comfortable. The tail curled around the arm shows how hard it is beating with excitement.

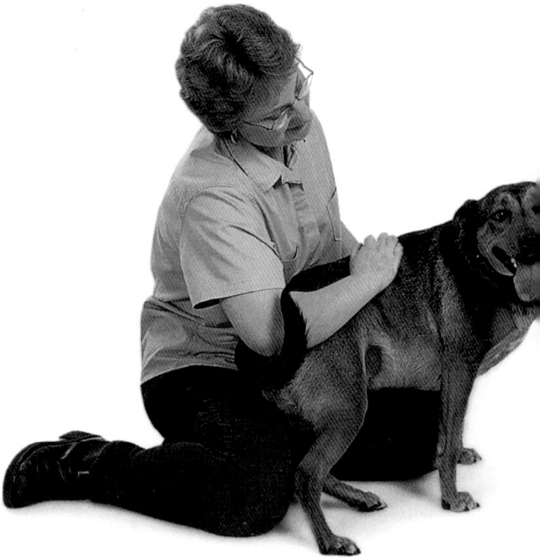

It's you!

This greyhound has recognized someone he knows and is excited. He has a relaxed face, 'kind' eyes, pulled-back mouth and ears and a wildly beating tail. Dogs that are greeting people sweep their tails from side to side in a wide arc. This dog is on a lead and cannot run forwards, so his front legs are sloping as he half bows in a gesture that is meant to entice the person he has seen to come closer to be with him. Most people recognize a greeting like this even though the mouth is open and the bottom teeth exposed, which may be misinterpreted as aggression.

Come closer

As his favourite person approaches, he has raised his paw in anticipation. He knows he cannot get closer because of the lead, so he puts his weight on his hind legs and gets ready to spring forward when she comes within range. He has the same 'smiling face and kind eyes' look that humans rarely misinterpret. Being an active hound, he is unlikely to want to be cuddled but instead will be inclined to race round and round his visitor, pushing against her every now and then so she can stroke him until his excitement and energy die down.

The importance of scent

A dog's primary sense is his sense of smell. Dogs have such an incredible sense of smell that they can find out all sorts of things about a person or place that we could never discover, just by sniffing. Scents linger for some time once they have been laid and, to a dog, sniffing is like watching a video of all the things that may have happened in that place in the past. Some owners get annoyed when their dog sniffs around things too much, but this is their main way of finding out about their world, in the same way that we find out what is happening in our immediate environment by using our primary sense of sight.

Who's been this way?

Your dog can find out a great deal of information by sniffing the urine and faeces left by other dogs. Although this procedure may be repellent to us, your dog can use it to discover who was recently in the area, how long ago they went past, whether they are male or female, well or unwell, their age, and what their breeding status is. In fact, gathering information by sniffing is so important to them that many dogs seem to be completely obsessed with it.

So that's where you've been

This dog is engrossed in sniffing the scents left by other dogs on this person's trousers as they have brushed against him. In the absence of any interesting smells on the trousers, dogs often sniff the groin area to take in the scent of the person they are investigating, which can be very embarrassing for owners and visitors who don't appreciate the intrusion!

DID YOU KNOW?

- ❑ The area in a dog's nose for detecting scent is nearly 37 times larger than that in humans.
- ❑ The parts of the brain that process signals coming in from the nose are far greater in size and complexity in a dog than are the corresponding parts of the human brain.

Oh yes, it's you

Cats like to rub the top of their heads on their friends. This cat is trying to do this to the dog, but the dog doesn't understand and takes the opportunity to sniff the cat's head instead. From this, he will be able to confirm that this is, indeed, his familiar friend, as well as being able to tell who has been stroking the cat and where he has been.

Meeting other dogs

Smell is very important in finding out about other dogs. One sniff saves them from having to ask how are you, where do you come from, what have you been eating, what sex are you, how old are you, and are you relaxed or frightened? It is likely that a dog can also tell many other things by sniffing which we just don't know about. Sniffing occurs in a ritualized way with both dogs in turn sniffing each other's mouth and rear end. After that, one dog may signal that he wants to play and a game will begin, or they will go their separate ways or even start to fight.

Who are you?

These dogs are restrained by their leads and can only reach to sniff nose to nose. Direct eye contact is avoided as this would be threatening. They approach very close to each other's teeth which could be very dangerous, but the behaviour is so ritualized that it usually goes without a hitch. Each dog will also have weighed up the other from a distance before going into such a close encounter. The Jack Russell on the right is a little put off by the intensity of the other dog's inquisitiveness and has responded by pulling herself up to her full height with her tail held high and ears pulled back.

DID YOU KNOW?

- Fearful dogs frequently find it difficult to read and send signals, which can often lead to fights.

So that's who you are

Sniffing the rear end must allow dogs to find out many things that they couldn't discover at the front as they spend a long time doing it, especially if they are uncastrated males. For creatures with such sensitive noses, they also need to get very close. Perhaps this is so that they get the scent message direct from its origin before it has decayed in the air or mixed with other scents.

Hold still so I can reach

Two dogs of very different sizes may have trouble sniffing each other at the same time and this may result in them turning round and round with each other until they have smelt enough. Sniffing the penis of male dogs seems to be important to them and usually induces a state of social inhibition of the dog being sniffed, which results in him staying completely still until the investigation is over.

Meeting people

Body language and signals play an important role in the lives of dogs, as they use their bodies to communicate their intentions and feelings in the same way that we use sounds and spoken language. These signals appear to be mostly inherited and instinctive, although the fine-tuning of when to use them most effectively has to be learned. Dogs will try to use the same signals during their interactions with humans as they do when 'talking' to each other, which can lead to all kinds of confusion between human and dog. Humans are guilty of doing this too.

Pleased to meet you

This dog wants to be friendly and is signalling this by his forward movement, his 'friendly' expression and by his attempts to lick the person's mouth. She recognizes this and wants to be friendly too, but being a human, she smiles, puts her hands on him, and moves her head so he can only lick her chin. Licking is an appeasement gesture that signals that he is no threat to her. He does this in the hope that she won't attack him as he doesn't know her well and is not completely sure of her character.

My special person

This dog has a special bond with an owner he has known since puppyhood, and licking the mouth has become a ritualized greeting. This action has its origins in the behaviour of puppies in the wild who would lick the mouths of adults returning to the nest to get them to regurgitate food they were carrying in their stomachs, something that is not likely to happen for pet dogs!

Hello, friend!

Dogs that know someone well will signal their greeting with their whole bodies. This dog strains against the lead to get to her friend, but her body is relaxed and not tense as it would be if she were about to display aggressive behaviour. Her tail is wagging in a big sweeping movement from side to side and her facial expression is a happy, silly 'grin'.

DID YOU KNOW?

- ❑ A wagging tail means that a dog is excited. It does not always mean that the dog is friendly, and it is important to read the rest of the body language before approaching a dog with a wagging tail.

I need to be up there with you

Dogs jump up to get closer to our faces. As puppies, they want to be close enough to lick our mouths. If this behaviour is rewarded when they are young, it becomes a habit later in life. This dog is anxious and excited, as shown by her wide mouth, pulled-back ears and protruding tongue, and is seeking reassurance from her owner. Having been told off for jumping up in the past, she is not fully committed to her action, and keeps her front paws low in case she needs to get down again quickly.

Can we be friends?

Whether or not two dogs will get on with each other will depend on many things such as how compatible their personalities are and how they are introduced. Some dogs are shy and worried about others, whereas some love to play and are happy to meet as many other dogs as possible. As with people, some dogs are good at social communication, but others often get into fights and squabbles because of a confusion over their intentions. Signalling and body language play a big role in these encounters.

I'm not sure about you

The Labrador does not have enough social skill or has too much drive to go forward to realize that the other dog is feeling a little overwhelmed by the speed of his approach. The brown-and-white dog holds his ground and sniffs briefly at the Labrador while avoiding eye contact. His ears are back indicating that he is concerned, and his tail is held in a neutral position so that he doesn't antagonize the other dog. The Labrador is very excited, as seen by his fast-moving, beating tail.

I'm still not sure about you

The rigid stance and the lack of reciprocal sniffing from the brown-and-white dog has had some effect on the behaviour of the Labrador. The hair at the base of the tail and along his back is beginning to rise, indicating that he is now a little worried too. His drive to investigate is still strong but he is less exuberant than before, and his front paw is raised in hesitation.

Let's have fun

After the sniffing is over, the dog on the left would like to be friends. The Jack Russell is still very rigid and tense, so the other dog tries a play-bow to try to entice her to relax and, perhaps, start a game. To do this, she puts her elbows to the ground and keeps her bottom in the air for a few seconds in the classic pose of a playful dog.

DID YOU KNOW?

❑ Signals, such as the play-bow, can be seen in dogs all around the world. Universal signals like these do not need to be learnt but can be recognized by dogs everywhere.

❑ Well-socialized dogs will have learnt how to fine-tune their behaviour so that they are readily accepted by other dogs.

Let's play!

This is the signal that says 'I would like to play with you'. Dogs will give this signal to humans as well as to other dogs. This pose will be held for a few seconds, with the tail beating furiously, before the dog jumps up and runs off, looking over his shoulder to see if his invitation to chase has been successful. This dog has learned to do this as a greeting and his relaxed 'smiling' face shows that a person he knows is coming near.

Dog talk

Compared to humans, dogs have a very limited ability to communicate using sound and tend to rely more on body language to get their message across. The range of sounds they produce tends to be used to back up their body language rather than in isolation. Howling and growling are the least common sounds, but barking is used frequently, often in different ways to convey different meanings. These can range from guarding barks to those designed to get attention, or barking can be used just to let off steam during excitement, or when feeling frustrated.

Can anyone hear me?

Howling is a good way to communicate with others who are far away. This husky is involved in a group howl and his howls have stimulated others to join in, each one on a different note. If separated from the rest of the pack, howling and waiting for others to respond helps the lost one to know in which direction to travel. Dogs kept in kennels will often howl as if to reunite themselves with members of their lost pack.

Stay away!

Keeping strangers away requires a deep, explosive series of barks, sometimes accompanied by a rush forward. This dog is showing his fear by flattening his ears against his head, by his mouth which is pulled back at the corners and by his big eyes, a result of the eyelids being held wide open. Cars are small spaces that are easily defended, and dogs often have more confidence about barking at strangers here than elsewhere.

Look at me! Look at me!

Barking designed to get attention is common in pampered small dogs that are doted on by their owners. This dog likes to be the centre of attention and when he feels he is being ignored, he will begin a long series of loud yaps, interspersed with short periods of quiet to give him time to recover. If his owner responds, he will stop; if not, he can continue in this way for an annoyingly long time!

Keep away from this!

A menacing growl can be very formidable and is designed to cast doubt in an opponent's mind about their ability to win the encounter. This dog is not going to lose his trophy easily and shows that he means business with a deep growl that is surprisingly loud for such a small dog. Anyone hearing this would find it difficult to ignore, and it is an obvious signal that it is dangerous to approach.

DID YOU KNOW?

- In comparison with human children, dogs are less able to understand sounds used as signals and find it quite hard to learn words such as 'sit' and 'come here'.
- It is much easier for a dog to learn spoken commands if these are given in conjunction with hand signals or gestures during training. The hand signal can be gradually withdrawn as the dog becomes better educated.

Life in a hierarchy

Dogs in a wild pack live in a social hierarchy in which they arrange themselves in status order beneath the leader. The biggest, strongest and smartest gain high status while the less able fill the subordinate roles. A hierarchical social structure ensures that the strongest dogs get the best food, access to the best sleeping places and the chance to breed and pass on their genes to the next generation.

You're my leader

Our dogs' ancestors, the wolves, have a very strong sense of hierarchy. This helps to reduce fighting within the pack, as each member knows their place and is careful not to overstep the mark. This is an important survival tool since each wolf is armed with a set of powerful jaws capable of inflicting terrible injury. Less fighting results in a fitter pack more capable of killing enough prey to survive.

You're all more important

Pet dogs are happiest when they see their role as lowest of the pack and are content to stay in that role. This dog has very little ambition to be leader and is happy to put all humans in the household, and even the cat, above himself. In this way, he remains a friendly, amiable pet who is happy to do whatever is asked of him and lets the humans take all responsibility for looking after him.

I'll go with you

This dog has grown up knowing that the children in the household are above her in status. She is happy to take direction from them and to be led in the direction they want her to go. This is despite the fact that she is far stronger than they are and able to pull her collar out of their grasp should she want to.

DID YOU KNOW?

❏ Good pack leaders look after the pack, ensuring they are well fed and comfortable. They don't always give in to demands and can be uncompromising and tough when necessary. They decide what to do and when to do it. They have sufficient strength to earn respect rather than constantly harassing or bullying to stay in control.

I'm higher than you

If two dogs live together, a hierarchy will develop between them. Being up high gives them an advantage and it is often used during disputes to help the leader win back control. Interestingly, it is often the physically smaller of a pair of litter mates who will take control. They often seem to have the bigger personality and more drive to be pack leader than their more relaxed larger sister or brother.

Who will be top dog?

Puppies will spend their first six months assessing the relative strengths and weaknesses of other members of the pack. They play with other puppies, and have many encounters with all pack members so that they can determine where their place in the pack lies. In a human family or when introduced to other dogs as adults, they have to go through a similar process to determine their status.

Am I stronger than you?

The puppy with the strongest will is likely to succeed, even against puppies that are physically stronger. Top dog status will not be decided until they reach puberty, but it may be clear quite quickly that one is mentally stronger than the other, is more persistent and wins more encounters.

During the next few months they will have many small competitions over toys or chews and they will play-fight together. By the time they reach adulthood, they will have a very clear idea of their status within the pack and with each other, and it is unlikely that they will need to fight again to prove it.

Let's play

Although they are having fun, playing helps to establish who has the best skills and ability and, hence, who is more able to lead the pack. Newly introduced dogs will play and interact together often, but this will gradually reduce as they get to know each other better.

Playing to win

This dog enjoys playing tug of war. He has strong jaws and an inborn desire to hold on to things and pull. Pushy dogs often play this game to find out if they are stronger than their competitors and to convince their opponent that they are more able to lead the pack. However, less ambitious dogs, like this one, may just be enjoying the game and are not trying to take control.

See if you can take it

The boxer's body language tells the collie that she is ready to defend the toy, and the collie had better be sure that she is strong enough to fight for it if she dares to try. Although this is play and there will be no serious consequences, being bold enough to try to succeed will make a difference to the establishment of hierarchy between them later.

DID YOU KNOW?

- The hierarchy in a wild dog pack is not fixed, but is fluid and will change if circumstances alter. Consequently, there is hope for humans whose dog has taken control of them!

I’m in charge

It is important for new leaders to impress on other pack members that they are in control. Although this is usually done by subtle means, it is sometimes necessary to convince those who are not yet subdued that the leader means business. Displays of aggression are, therefore, not uncommon in newly formed or unstable packs, particularly if the leader is struggling to hold on to the top spot.

You will obey me!

There is no mistaking the intentions of this husky. He is top dog in the pack and one of his subordinates has been brave enough to question his authority. The challenger is treated to unblinking, piercing eye contact and a full display of teeth. The tongue is sticking out and is held rigid in a dominant display of hostility. The body is forward, ready to attack, and is drawn up to its full height to impress on the adversary just how formidable his opponent is. This posture is often accompanied by a deep, rumbling growl.

See how big my teeth are!

During conflicts, this expression is designed to display the weaponry that your dog possesses. The lips are drawn up in front as far as they will go, which means that the corners of the mouth are brought forward rather than drawn back as in a fearful dog. This is a deliberate display of strength and you are being given the chance to back down. Any retreat needs to be slow and obvious to avoid triggering an attack.

I have the top dog spot

In an established pack, displays of strength, if needed, are often much more subtle than open aggression. Being first up onto the chair, taking toys up there and using your body to block any attempts the other dog makes to get up are good ways to reinforce your position as leader without the need to get nasty. Aggression is also less likely to occur in pet dogs as life is usually quite easy and they are often neutered so there is less need for them to be competitive.

Hello, I'm your friend

A submissive 'grin' like this is often misinterpreted by humans, who think the dog is being aggressive. In reality, these 'grins' are similar to a human smile and are often shown when the dog is greeting people he knows or is being told off. Strangely, these 'grins' are usually reserved solely for humans rather than other dogs, and the propensity to show this behaviour seems to be inherited and to run in families.

Okay, you win

Once the pack is formed, subordinates will display their lower status more often than those in higher-ranking positions demonstrate their superiority. They do this by frequent displays of submission whenever they come into contact with a higher-ranking animal. These submissive actions provide the oil that keeps a hierarchy running smoothly. They prevent leaders from getting aggressive to show that they are in charge – something that is appreciated by every member of the pack.

See how unimportant I am

This dachshund has learnt that her place is at the bottom of the pack. Rolling on her back, exposing her belly and leaving herself totally vulnerable displays her complete acceptance of the higher-ranking pack member's ability to decide her fate. An attack is unlikely on one who lays themselves open so completely. This strategy is a good one and often gets her out of situations where she would otherwise receive a telling off; hence she looks relaxed and comfortable.

I'm just a puppy, no need to attack

This puppy has just met this big dog for the first time. Instinctively he knows that a display of submission may prevent an attack. Raising a front paw, flicking out his tongue and exposing his belly all help in the race to say he is not worth bothering with. The puppy is not sure if this strategy will work, hence he is a little apprehensive as may be seen by his pulled-back ears, wide mouth and raised head.

I bow to your superiority

This dog is worried about being on the receiving end of a prolonged stare. He is not sure of the person's intentions and so has lowered his head and is raising a paw. A paw raised in submission is not being offered to hold. People often think the dog is trying to shake hands and reach out to reciprocate. The lowering of the head indicates that the teeth are out of action and you are not in any danger.

DID YOU KNOW?

❑ Submissive puppies and even adult dogs may produce a small amount of urine when greeting higher-ranking members of the pack or family to give a smelly clue that they are not a threat.

Give me a treat

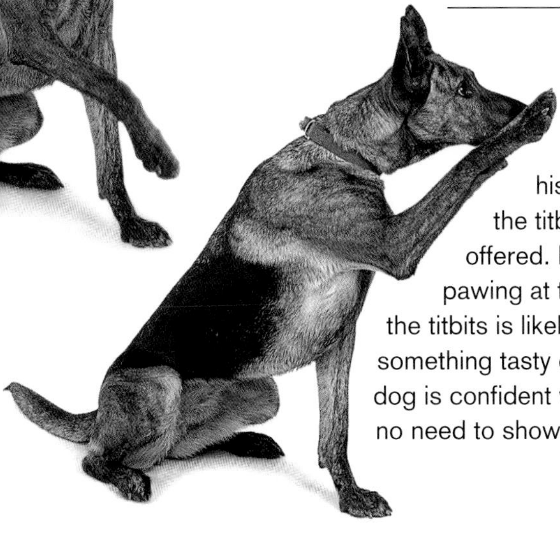

This dog has a different reason for raising his paw. His head is up and his senses focused on the titbit that is being offered. He has learnt that pawing at the person holding the titbits is likely to result in something tasty coming his way. This dog is confident with people and sees no need to show submission.

Giving in and challenges

How dogs view their status with humans will not be determined by encounters they have with other dogs. They will base their judgement on a separate assessment of the human's strengths and capabilities rather than on their success with other dogs. By the time a puppy reaches six months old, or after an adult dog has been in its new home for about two weeks, it will have made an assessment of where it fits into the family.

After you

This dog is happy to be second to go through the door and waits patiently. Dogs that think they deserve high status will barge past their owners, trying to be first into the room. Small contests like this often go unnoticed by owners who have more important things on their minds, but, to an ambitious dog, they are a further indication that he should be in charge.

I want to go this way

Dogs that always get their own way will think that life revolves around them so they must be important. Always giving in to your dog's demands will give him an artificial view of his status. Going your own way and, perhaps later, allowing him to do what he wanted to do as a reward for complying with your direction will help him to accept his place in your family.

Get past me if you can

Dogs often display their high status by preventing pack members from moving freely around the territory. They may need to use aggression to stop wayward pack members ignoring their 'rules'. Challenges like this one are frightening for owners and likely to lead to success for the dog. Previous smaller challenges, often unnoticed by owners and won by the dog, will have given the dog the confidence to risk such a major display of strength.

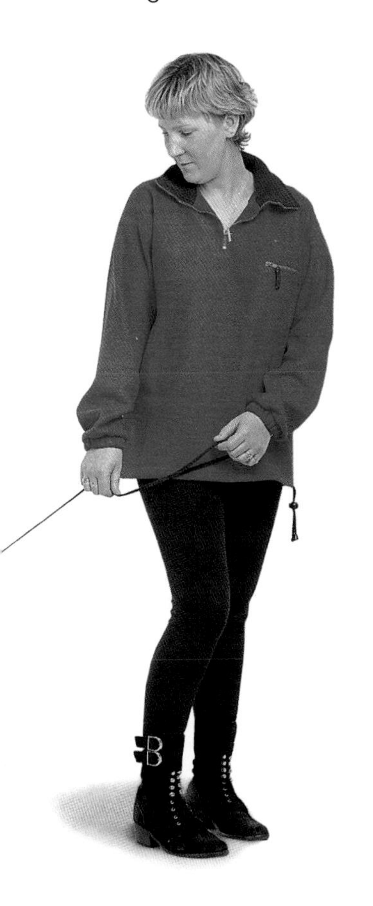

DID YOU KNOW?

- ❑ Acquiring high status is mostly based on winning small encounters with pack members rather than risking defeat during bigger challenges.
- ❑ Being pushy and attempting to get your own way at all times is likely to wear down the competition so that they give in to your demands, unless they are similarly ambitious themselves.
- ❑ Since dogs are looking at controlling different resources than humans, their bid for power often goes unnoticed until it is too late.

Food and fitness

Dogs descended from animals that made their living by hunting large prey in packs. Although we have domesticated them and selectively bred them until they no longer resemble their wild ancestors, they still retain many of the characteristics that make them efficient hunters. The hunting sequence can be broken down into components – scent trail, watch, stalk, chase, grab, bite, shake, kill, consume – all of which can be seen at different times in our own docile pets.

I'm coming to get you

Predatory behaviour in wolves is strong and instinctive. All of this wolf's senses are focused on his prey as he stalks closer. His body is held as still as possible to avoid detection and he is ready to seize the opportunity to make a successful chase. This is an unacceptable trait in pet dogs but nonetheless present in some domestic dogs. Unfortunately, it is an inbred characteristic that cannot be removed. However, in most dogs, if training is started early enough in their lives, it can be controlled.

Come here, little rabbit

Greyhounds have been bred with the ability and desire to catch small things that run, like this rabbit. This is an unacceptable trait in pet dogs whose owners may even own a pet rabbit themselves. The strength of the predatory trait varies and some greyhounds take no notice. Others will patiently wait for their opportunity.

Slowly, slowly, catchy piggy!

This Ridgeback's predatory instincts began to develop when she was about six months old. Although her behaviour is strongly inhibited by her owner and the sow, both of whom are nearby, she cannot resist stalking these young piglets, which would make a tasty meal. She has never had to catch her own food, but her instinct to hunt is so strong that she risks getting into trouble to do so. She moves slowly, so as not to scare them, with all her senses fixed on her victim, oblivious to everything else around her.

DID YOU KNOW?

- Different breeds of dog have been bred to exploit different elements of the hunting sequence. Hounds are bred to track and trail, herding dogs to chase and terriers to catch and kill.

Watch and wait

A collie's drive to eye, stalk and chase have been selected for over the generations until they display these behaviours readily. Each of these behaviours has a different use while working sheep, and all are highly valued in the working sheepdog. In the wild, watching and waiting to see whether prey are moving and in which direction gives essential information that may result in a more successful hunt.

Going to catch you

A dog's desire to chase is legendary and man has utilized it to produce the dogs used to herd sheep and cattle. The genes responsible have been passed to our pet dogs and the trait is particularly strong in those that are descended from herding stock. If this desire is not channelled into acceptable games with toys, dogs can pick up many bad habits and get into a great deal of trouble for carrying out inappropriate chases.

Got to catch him

Border collies are among the best chasers in the world. This dog is excited by the man running past and gives chase. He is a friendly dog and his intention is not to bite the man, but to catch up with him. However, some dogs will nip when they get close, especially if they are very excited by the chase or are scared of strangers. Since people can become scared or hurt by this behaviour, it is essential to divert it into games with toys instead.

DID YOU KNOW?

- ❑ Dogs in a pack are more likely to chase and hunt than a single dog on its own.
- ❑ Two dogs are enough to form a pack and, together, they will be brave and bold enough to try things that they wouldn't have the courage to do alone.
- ❑ This can be a real problem for owners of more than one dog, especially if the dogs enjoy chasing things they shouldn't, such as bikes or joggers.

I can run faster

Cars run away quickly and present the perfect chance for a good fast chase. This dog is at full stretch and is running as fast as she can. Some dogs become so obsessed with car chasing that they will continue even after they have experienced an accident that leaves them seriously injured. This is a dangerous game to play as both dog and people can easily be injured or killed.

Let me get it

This dog has learnt to enjoy chasing the light beam from a torch. Played since early puppyhood, it is one of her favourite games. With the torch held by a child in the family, the beam moves fast and erratically, sometimes shining onto the ceiling out of reach and sometimes racing across the carpet and onto chairs and walls. Since she is more interested in chasing than catching, this is an exciting and fulfilling game for her, although she is oblivious to everything when chasing and risks damaging herself on furniture or other obstacles that get in the way.

Catching up

If dogs do not have enough opportunities to chase after toys, they will find another outlet for their energy by giving chase to anything that moves fast. Dogs that have descended from working stock often have much more energy than their owners realize and they are often left understimulated and waiting for action. This can frequently lead to unacceptable behaviour in one form or another. More regular sessions of exciting chase games with toys is usually the most practical answer to preventing or reducing this type of problem.

I've nearly got it

Dogs with nothing to chase in their environment may resort to chasing the only thing that moves – their tail. This can become an obsession and they can become oblivious to everything around them as they circle and spin. Sometimes they catch it and can make it bleed, but the important part is the chase as, even if their tail is amputated, they will continue to chase the stump. Providing a more stimulating environment and more games with toys can provide the dog with a more fulfilling life.

DID YOU KNOW?

- ❑ Some dogs prefer toys that roll as they like a long chase, whereas others prefer toys that are shaped to bounce erratically, as these simulate the twists and turns of live prey.
- ❑ Balls on ropes that can be spun in a circle and let go, or toys that come with a device that propels them further than humans can throw can provide longer chases that will be appreciated by very active dogs.

Go on, move again

Some dogs are fascinated by the activities of other pets within the home. Although they make unsuitable playmates, this dog enjoys watching the rat's movement and will give chase if allowed to or if she gets the opportunity. This may have disastrous consequences for the other pet, and it is best to prevent these interests developing from the outset and refocus your dog's attention onto games with toys instead. This is not difficult to do, since games with toys that can be caught and chewed are often more satisfying anyway.

This is fun

Chasing children in the household is fun as they move fast and erratically, and often make exciting noises as they are chased. This is enjoyable for the dog, but if uncontrolled can get out of hand quickly. Also, if the dog learns to do this at home, he will be likely to chase unfamiliar children outside in the park or street. Encouraging children to play with the dog with toys is a better solution and will prevent the dog from getting into trouble later on.

Caught you

Once the dog has caught up with the prey, the next part of the hunting sequence is to dispatch it as quickly as possible with a pounce, grab and a killing bite. Although our pet dogs do not have such strong predatory instincts as their ancestors, they retain some of the characteristics that would enable them to be successful predators in the wild. Most dogs enjoy grabbing a toy at the end of a chase and some of them will then bite it hard and shake it vigorously, simulating the killing of their prey.

You're mine now

This toy is being dragged along the ground and is jumping about like a small animal. The collie pounces on it, using his front feet to hold it still until he can get hold of it with his teeth. Dogs will use the pounce to stun small prey, especially if they are hidden in undergrowth, as this action will prevent the prey from running away. For larger prey they use the grabbing bite only.

Got it

Grabbing the ball at the end of the chase is satisfying and is enjoyed by most dogs. This terrier grabs the toy and closes his strong jaws several times, causing the toy to squeak loudly. Although only a game, it satisfies the innate hunting drives and this dog is less likely to go out looking for prey.

DID YOU KNOW?

- Terriers were originally bred to catch and kill small animals such as rats and other creatures considered to be vermin. Their predatory instinct is strong, which is why they enjoy playing with squeaky toys that simulate the squeaks of captured prey.

Let's give it a shake

Shaking vigorously can stun prey or cause them fatal injuries, making it less likely that they will fight back. This dog has strong neck muscles, enabling him to shake his head so fast that the loose skin of his lips and eyes is left behind. Although practising on toys improves a dog's hunting skills, this is preferable to trying to stop him fulfilling his desire to carry out this natural behaviour altogether as this is unlikely to be successful.

Let me eat you

Most pet dogs are fed on a diet that requires very little chewing. However, they have not lost the ancient desires that would have enabled them to chew through the thick skin of large prey and chew up every last bit of the carcass. For this reason, dogs enjoy chewing their toys to pieces and exercising their jaws on chews and bones. In the absence of anything acceptable to chew, they may destroy household objects or children's toys, so it is sensible for dog owners to provide a range of suitable items instead, such as rawhide chews or deep-fried bones or sinews.

I need to chew you up

Once captured and 'killed', the next stage is to chew open the 'carcass'. This dog uses his paws to turn the now squeakless hedgehog until its nose is uppermost as this is the easiest bit to chew off.

You have tough skin

Sometimes skin and sinews, or in this case, plastic, can be tough, and you need strong muscles to pull the meat from the bones. By standing up and placing his front paws on the toy, this dog can get a good leverage that will enable him to pull pieces off. If these were meat they would be eaten, but, instead, they are spat out.

DID YOU KNOW?

- Bones and chews keep dogs happy for hours as they provide interest and exercise for jaws.
- Rawhide chews are sometimes too hard for dogs to enjoy chewing. Soaking one end in water to soften it makes them more palatable and a lot easier to chew.
- Dogs should always have a variety of chews available in order to prevent them from chewing rugs, furniture or any other things they shouldn't.

I like to chew

Even old dogs like to chew, a fact that is often overlooked by owners who think dogs need to chew only during puppyhood. Since the ancestors of our dogs would have needed to be able to chew tough carcasses throughout their lives, our pets have had this trait passed down to them too. Dogs that were bred specifically to use their mouths to carry game, such as Labradors and other gundogs, are even more likely to enjoy chewing than other breeds.

So much energy

The ancestors of our pet dogs, the wolves, travelled vast distances looking for herds of prey animals. Humans selectively bred dogs to do active jobs for them such as herding sheep or flushing out game, most of which required a high level of stamina. As a result, most of the dogs we now keep as pets are descended from animals that could keep going all day, even though we now usually want them to be inactive for most of it.

Going up!

Once they have learnt to do it, fit, active dogs love to jump onto things. They seem to enjoy the challenge of getting up there, exercising their bodies as they do so. They often don't need a reason and do it just because they can.

It's good to run

Greyhounds are built for speed. Fit young dogs like this one love to run and will often do so when first released just to use up excess energy that has built up. Greyhounds prefer short bursts of speed to a slower jogging that can be kept up all day, and often run themselves nearly to exhaustion before laying down for a while to recharge their batteries.

DID YOU KNOW?

- As pets, we expect our dogs to lay quietly for long periods and make do with just a few short walks. Sadly for them, this goes against their natural drives.
- Many behavioural problems arise because our pet dogs have too much energy and try to find their own entertainment in ways that we wish they would not.

Got to get there faster

Dogs pull on the lead because they want to travel faster than their owner. Even if the owner runs, it will not be fast enough as dogs want to travel even faster. By pulling into the collar, they think they will achieve their aim to get there quicker. The forward movement of the owner reinforces this behaviour and the dog, thinking he has been successful, does it even more.

I can run faster

Dogs love to play chase games with each other as it uses up energy and makes them feel good. The brown dog has taken the lead and the sheepdog is running as fast as he can to catch up.

Life is great

Dogs that have all their needs met are more contented and better behaved than those that are constantly trying to use up unexpended energy. For fit, young and active dogs there is a variety of ways in which to do this, all of which involve both physical and mental activity. Owners who make an effort to play with their dogs on a regular basis often enjoy the additional advantage of having a better relationship with them.

Got to get that toy

Playing with toys is a good way to redirect energy into harmless activity. This dog has all senses focused on the toy and is totally engrossed in trying to catch it. By doing so, he is exercising both mind and body. Since the person is the source of all the fun, the game can be used to build a bond between them.

Got it!

With a bit of practice, dogs are as good at catching things in their mouths as we are at catching with our hands. This dog has had to leap off the ground to get his mouth into the correct position, but has managed to connect with the ball even though it is travelling with incredible speed. (When playing these sorts of games with inexperienced dogs, it is important to ensure that the ball is too large to be swallowed.)

Over!

Agile collies like this one have no problem jumping once they have learnt to do so. This dog is kept busy with agility and obedience practice by her owner and, consequently, is relaxed and happy around the house. Dogs that are boisterous and overpowering at home often have too much energy and they would be nicer to live with if they were given more play and more exercise.

DID YOU KNOW?

- Toys are good substitute prey since they can become objects to be searched for in long grass, to be chased and caught, and to be fought over in a tug-of-war game.
- Some dogs bury their toys as a way of keeping them safe for another day.

Let me get it

This basset hound has a build that makes it impossible for him to be as active as other dogs. His short legs, heavy body, and excess skin make it difficult for him to jump around and play. However, playing football with his friend is an easy way to use up the little bit of energy he has and he enjoys the thrill of the chase, albeit a short one.

Hunters and scavengers

Dogs in the wild have three strategies they employ for finding enough food. They can hunt large prey in packs, hunt for smaller prey alone or scavenge for leftover food or dead carcasses. Which one of these they choose will depend upon the environment in which they find themselves, but their genetic make-up has equipped them with the drives and abilities to allow them to do all three. Hunting may be the best option if prey are sufficiently numerous, whereas scavenging may be a better strategy if they live in close proximity to wasteful humans.

Most pet dogs get food handed to them on a plate once or twice a day and never have to find their own food. Humans often feel that, because of this, there is no need for them to hunt or scavenge, and often punish them for doing so. However, until we breed dogs that have very little remaining of the genetics of their ancestors, dogs will continue to have the drives and desires that allowed their predecessors to acquire enough to eat.

Oh, this is nice

In order to hunt successfully, it is better if your prey cannot detect your presence until the last moment. For a smelly animal like a wolf or dog, this can be difficult. For this reason, it is sensible to cover yourself in any strong-smelling substance that is in your environment. This dog has found some fox droppings which have a particularly strong odour and is rolling on them to try to cover her shoulder and back regions with scent. This appears to give her lots of pleasure and she continues to do it until she attracts the attention of another dog that comes over to join in.

Move over and let me join in

The Weimaraner has spotted the fun and has come to join in. He too rolls around on his back to cover himself in the exotic perfume. To the human nose, this smell is particularly repugnant and this behaviour will, more often than not, result in a good bath once the dog gets home. Once sweet-smelling again, the urge to find another strong odour to roll in on the next walk is very strong.

Ah ha, food!

Dogs have no inhibitions about eating food when they can. Humans find this raiding or stealing behaviour annoying and try to instill some sense of wrongdoing in their dog when they find this has happened. However, a dog that takes food when it is available is likely to be much more successful in a world where it may never know where the next meal is coming from. Humans, therefore, are fighting against ancient drives to be opportunistic.

This is my food

In the wild, an animal often has to compete with others to get enough to eat. Once they have obtained a piece of food, it is important to hang on to it. If it is lost, it may mean going hungry. So motivation to keep hold of it is strong. Possession seems to be all-important and small dogs will often guard food from dogs that are much larger, stronger or higher ranking.

Stay away from my bone

This large meaty bone is a good prize for this little dog that is usually fed a bland diet. She has lots of confidence that she will be able to keep hold of it, having had encounters like this in the past. Her whole body has stiffened and she is ready to bite. Her lips are drawn back to signal her intentions and she is emitting a deep rumbling growl.

Just you try to take it

Guarding a chew to stop it being taken away by another dog is easy for this Ridgeback. She has had lots of previous encounters with her competitor and has always won. All that is necessary to make him back off is a piercing stare and a dazzling display of teeth. Knowing that she is likely to succeed, she is not protecting the chew further by covering it with her head and body.

DID YOU KNOW?

- Despite getting plenty of food to eat each day, many dogs will defend valued food items such as chews, bones, tasty titbits or even the food in their dish.
- Possessiveness often begins in the litter when puppies have to fight between themselves to get enough to eat or keep hold of valuable resources.
- To prevent this from happening, dogs need to learn that hands come to give not take. If this is taught to them from an early age, they no longer feel the need to keep us away from what they have.

I'll just take this out of your way

The large dog is obviously bigger and stronger than the little dogs but, even so, he is worried that they may try to steal his bone. These three dogs live in an amiable pack and rather than risk confrontation, the large dog decides to move the bone to a safer place before chewing it. Dogs that choose this option are safer to have around than those that are quick to use maximum aggression in order to defend a valued possession.

Saving some for later

In the wild, food isn't always in plentiful supply. Occasionally, however, there is too much to eat in one go and the surplus must be stored safely so that it is available in times of hunger. Carrying and burying excess meat from a kill, therefore, makes sense in a world of unpredictable food supply as it can be dug up and consumed later. Dogs have powerful digestive systems that can cope with rotting and decaying meat. Their stomachs contain powerful enzymes that allow them to eat decomposing meat without becoming ill.

Must save this for later

This big bone cannot be enjoyed all at once and now that this dog has had enough for the time being, the rest must be stored for another time. This trait of carrying food home to bury for later or to feed puppies has been selectively bred for in retrievers and other gundogs. Humans exploit their desire to carry food but not to eat it.

Where did I leave that bone?

Some dogs seem to know exactly where they have buried their bones and others seem to forget. Unless the bone is buried very deeply, your dog's keen sense of smell will help him locate it. Test holes in the flowerbed are not always welcomed by keen gardeners but dogs respond to a deeply felt urge to retrieve their cache from time to time.

Coming to get you

Your dog may dig for reasons other than to bury bones. This dog is digging in the soft earth of a molehill. Once she has reached the tunnels left by the mole, she stops and breathes in deeply, hoping to catch the scent of her prey. She does not realize that, even if it were not long gone, the mole could escape down its tunnels more quickly than she could dig.

Got to catch them

Some terriers were bred to be small and good at digging so that they could catch rabbits, foxes and other animals that live down holes. This dog has some terrier ancestry and enjoys digging in the water. His activity splashes up small, fast-moving droplets of water that make the game even more fun as he tries to catch them.

DID YOU KNOW?

- Dogs prefer to bury excess food in private and, if disturbed, will often take the bone or chew away to bury elsewhere.
- The urge to save excess food can be strong and dogs deprived of soft earth in which to bury things will often go through the motions of pushing soil around it with their noses, even if it is on paving slabs or carpet.
- In the absence of excess food or bones, toys and chews are frequently buried substitutes.

Taking a nap

Dogs like to be comfortable when they sleep and will search for a safe place at the right temperature. Dogs spend quite a lot of time sleeping, especially as they get older, but do not necessarily sleep all night as we generally expect them to do in our homes. Providing puppies and young dogs with something to do when they wake up can help to prevent disturbed sleep for the human inhabitants of the household.

I shouldn't be up here

Sofas, with their comfortable, squashy cushions, are great places for dogs to rest. Unfortunately for them, their owners often have other ideas about where they should sleep and tell them off. This dog is not supposed to be here and her expression shows that she is expecting to be told to get down at any moment.

DID YOU KNOW?

❑ Many dogs prefer to sleep underneath some form of protection such as a table, bed or behind the sofa. This could be linked to the trait of 'going to ground' in times of danger when puppies were raised in dens.

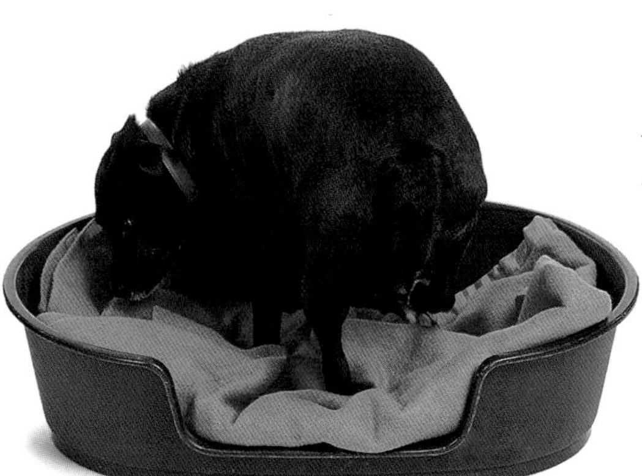

Got to get comfortable

Your dog likes to be comfortable when he sleeps and this is not possible if his bedding is sticking up in places. Before settling, many dogs turn round and round, as this one is doing, to flatten out any lumps and bumps.

I wish this blanket would flatten

This action would have worked well when the bedding was dry grasses or earth, but is less effective on the soft blankets and dog beds that we give our pets today. If the sleeping area is still not comfortable enough, some raking with the front paws may be necessary. This may be done even on unyielding carpet as your dog goes through ancient actions designed to make himself a soft bed.

At last ...!

Finally he lies down comfortably, but he is not yet relaxed enough to sleep and keeps his eyes open for further action or in case there are more exciting things to do.

Staying cool

Keeping your body at an optimum temperature is an important task for all mammals. Temperature receptors in the body let a dog know when he is cooling down and heating up and then some action must be taken. Like us, dogs enjoy lying in sunny spots to warm up or find shade to cool down. Overheating or cooling down too much can result in injury to the body and so behaviour to avoid the problem has quite a high priority.

It's cooler here

Having a black coat means that you heat up quicker on sunny days. This dog has moved into the shade of a tree to keep cool. Failure to do so would mean a rapid rise in his body temperature which could become dangerous on very hot days. Inactivity also stops the body from heating up further and, like us, dogs are likely to become more sluggish when the weather is warmer.

DID YOU KNOW?

- ❑ Unlike us, dogs do not sweat through glands in the skin (except through a few in their feet). Instead, they cool down by rapidly forcing cooling air over the surface of their tongue. Blood vessels on the surface expand, giving it a bright pink colour. Water evaporates from the tongue, helping to cool the dog down further.
- ❑ The further out of the mouth the tongue is, the hotter the dog.
- ❑ Stress panting tends to be faster than that designed to cool them down with shorter breaths being taken each time, and the tongue does not stick so far out of the mouth.

Nice breeze here

Long-haired dogs have a special problem in trying to stay cool. We have selectively bred certain breeds for excessively long-haired coats, often in countries where it acts as protection from a cold climate, and then transported these dogs around the world to live in hotter places. Hot dogs will often lie in doorways where the moving air currents help to keep them cool. Another reason for lying in doorways is in order to control the movement of other pack members around the territory if the dog is aiming to achieve high status in the social structure.

Nice and warm

Conservatories in winter are an ideal place in which to catch a few rays of warming sun. Being too cold is as bad as being too hot and uses up vital energy as the dog's body tries to generate the necessary heat, so finding warm places to lie when the weather is cold is a sensible survival strategy. Dogs seem to enjoy stretching out in the sun but, like us, they are liable to suffer from sunburn on exposed skin, particularly if they have white coats.

The next generation

The urge to reproduce and pass their genes on to the next generation is strong in unneutered dogs. Both bitches and dogs will be strongly motivated to get to each other at the appropriate time. Bitches come into season twice a year and during this time both male and female will try very hard to find ways to get together to mate, overcoming all obstacles to produce the next generation of puppies. This is one of the reasons why there are too many dogs for the number of good homes available. Having your pet neutered is a good way to ensure not only that they are not contributing to the numbers of unwanted animals, but also that they do not display a range of undesirable and inconvenient behaviours that are associated with the powerful urge to find a mate.

This fence can't stop me

Male dogs are particularly difficult to keep confined if there is a bitch in season nearby. Getting to her becomes all-important and they will risk life and limb to ensure they reach her. This may involve jumping high fences, as the motivation is strong and will give them the impetus they need to try it. Dogs that cannot get out often go off their food or pace and whine in frustration. This active young male has strong hind legs and can scale the fence easily from a standing start.

One solution to this problem is castration which gets rid of the motivation to escape and takes away the frustration. It will have no effect, however, if there are other reasons for trying to get out such as boredom.

DID YOU KNOW?

❏ At the time of peak receptivity for females, which occurs about one week into the season, they will become as anxious to get to males as they are to get to her and will try hard to reach them. Once the season is over bitches can be spayed, which takes away the desire to escape and mate, and prevents the risk of unwanted puppies in the future.

Got to get to her

Secure fences are no match for this little dog as he squeezes through a small hole dug underneath. For small dogs, going underneath or through is often easier than going over. Male dogs can smell the pheromones produced by a bitch in season from a distance of up to five kilometres (three miles) – it is no wonder that a bitch may attract a large gathering of likely suitors at this time.

Nearly there

Unneutered male dogs will cover long distances in search of females with which to mate. Even if they cannot detect any in their area, the urge to mate is strong and can drive them far from home. If they are not caught by a dog warden, or handed in to a police station, they may eventually return in a poor state – very thin and with sore feet and a tangled coat – having accomplished their mission.

May the best man win

Competition between male dogs on the same territory is strong, with each hoping to outdo the others so that he may be the one to mate with available females. Long before they get to meet face to face, dogs will be aware of rivals on their territory from the scent messages they leave. In return they leave their own, hoping that other dogs will realize from their scent that they are the biggest and strongest in the area.

Here's my message

This male dog lifts his leg to aim his stream of urine as high as possible so that others will be able to smell it easily. Dogs that are marking their territory will leave just a little urine in many strategic places on a walk, rather than leaving a lot in one place. Owners often become annoyed at having to stop so frequently to allow this to happen. Prominent objects along the route will be marked, often after the dog has sniffed thoroughly at another dog's mark that has been left there.

Who went past here?

Chemicals in the urine tell your dog how long ago the other dog passed and what its age, sex and status is. He can spend quite a long time investigating a scent. If it is a strong or interesting smell, he sometimes uses a special scent/taste organ at the roof of his mouth to help him get more information. When he does this, he will open his mouth slightly and chatter his teeth together as he sucks the scent into his mouth.

I'll show him ...

This male dog has sniffed the scent of a rival, overmarked the spot with his own urine and is now raking the ground with his feet. This allows him to spread his own scent more strongly by using the glands between his pads. As well as leaving a scent message, this action is often a strong visual signal of challenge and may be done also as a display of strength to warn rivals not to take him on.

DID YOU KNOW?

❑ Competition between males for the right to breed begins in earnest during puberty at about six to seven months of age.

❑ During adolescence, levels of male hormone are far greater than those in adult males, making them 'supercharged' in their desire to compete.

... how big and strong I am!

Grass is often raked up and flung up during this display, further adding to the powerful image. The dog's tail is held high, showing his confidence, and his mouth is open with excitement. If the other dog is present, he may try to hold eye contact while he does this as a gesture of threat and intimidation. In a neutered male dog, this display may be an attempt to keep other dogs at a distance and shows that he does not have the required social skills to deal with unfamiliar dogs at close quarters.

Seeing off rivals

Eventually, rival males will come into contact with each other. During these encounters, there will be much posturing and many interactions designed to find out which dog is more able to win the competition. This may involve rough play or can result in fighting if both dogs are of similar strength and neither is prepared to back down. Serious fighting can result in injury but it is worth it for the winner if he secures his right to breed.

I'm top dog here

The black dog has pulled himself up to his full height, has raised his tail and challenges the collie with direct eye contact. Not to be outdone, the collie stiffens, returns the eye contact and raises his tail, although not as high. The black dog seems to have gained the upper hand at the moment, and the collie needs to decide whether to return the challenge or back down.

I'm bigger than you

The Weimaraner knows how big and powerful he is and tries to show the black dog that he is a better competitor with a ritualized mounting behaviour. Similar to the mounting action used when mating, this is a rude, uninvited action that other dogs do not like. The Weimaraner is young, active but not that confident, and has chosen this action in preference to posturing. The black dog swivels his head around and bares his teeth in a gesture of defiance.

Oh no you don't

The black dog is now back in control and shows the Weimaraner that he means business with an obvious display of teeth. His confidence has been dented slightly, as shown by his lowered tail and his body posture which is lower than when he was dealing with the collie. The Weimaraner opens his mouth in a play biting gesture, but moves his head away with eyes averted showing that he does not want the encounter to get too serious. The black dog's strengths are confidence and experience while the Weimaraner has youth, exuberance and physical strength.

DID YOU KNOW?

- Since passing on your genes to the next generation is important, fights can turn nasty with serious injuries sometimes being inflicted if they are allowed to continue. Fights will also be more serious if there is a bitch in season nearby as the motivation will be stronger.

While you are busy ...

While the Weimaraner is occupied trying to pin the black dog to the ground, the sandy-coloured dog seizes the opportunity to practise mounting behaviour. Being young, he is no match for these two, but, excited by the competition, he seizes his chance to outdo the dog that he thinks will be the most likely victor.

Bringing up the babies

The purpose of male competition is to mate with bitches on the territory as they come into season. The resulting puppies are raised predominantly by the mother, who cares for them until they are old enough to join the rest of the pack. Although her maternal behaviour is instinctive, she will get better at it as she gains experience. Actions such as severing the umbilical cord when the puppies are first born, allowing them to suckle and cleaning them are all natural behaviours which are done without any need for learning or experience, although they do get better after several litters.

Hold still

This Ridgeback shows the classic pose of a dog mounting a bitch. However, she is a bitch herself and the purpose of her behaviour is to remind the other bitch in her pack who is in charge. This dominating action is a less aggressive way to keep control than fighting and she does this whenever the Springer takes liberties that she considers inappropriate for her status in the pack. This action subdues the Springer for a while and has the desired effect of re-establishing the Ridgeback's role as leader.

DID YOU KNOW?

- ❑ Smell plays an important role in a mother's behaviour and her recognition of the puppies.
- ❑ Puppies are sometimes rejected by their mother if they are born by Caesarean and cleaned up before being given back to her as she comes round from the anaesthetic.
- ❑ Puppies can be rejected by stressed mothers if they are handled by unfamiliar people too soon and do not smell like her own puppies when they are given back to her.

Let me clean you

The mother licks the puppy to stimulate it to go to the toilet. Until the puppies are old enough to move away from the nest to be clean, she will continue to do this after each feed, swallowing their waste products to keep the nest hygienic, thereby controlling disease and reducing the risk of attracting predators.

Is there any food in there?

Puppies instinctively lick at the corners of the mouth of adults. Although domestic dogs rarely regurgitate food for puppies, their ancestors would carry food home in their stomachs and deliver it to the puppies on request. Mouth-licking behaviour is regularly shown to humans too and puppies will jump up to try to reach our faces. If this behaviour is rewarded with attention from the puppy's owner, the bad habit of jumping up is developed from an early age.

Staying safe

Dogs are equipped with strong teeth and jaws that can inflict serious injuries and, consequently, have developed an elaborate body language to display their feelings and intentions to each other. They frequently use these signals with us but, being human, we often ignore them or fail to respond to them because we don't understand what they mean or, worse still, misinterpret them.

It's too intense

Yawning is often one of the first signs that your dog is uneasy about a situation. He may be in conflict within himself, trying to decide whether or not to move away, or he could be signalling to you that he is not happy. Dogs will often yawn when people stare at them and call their name. Humans frequently mistakenly think they are tired and take no notice of this important signal.

I'm feeling uneasy

Dogs will flick out their tongue when they feel uneasy or unsettled. They will lick their nose or just flick their tongue in and out quickly. This dog's nose-lick signals that she is not as relaxed as she appears. She has rolled over on her back to expose her belly in a gesture of appeasement, but the nose-licking shows that it is tinged with apprehension.

I don't like this

In response to this person's continued stare, this dog is looking anxious. His large pupils and drawn-back eyelids and ears show that he is getting worried. He keeps an eye on her out of the corner of his eye rather than giving her a direct look that could be perceived as threatening. His body is tense and his tail is down.

Perhaps this will make it obvious

Slowly and gradually, he turns his back on her and faces the other way. His tail is tucked under and he is still tense but, for the moment, he has relieved the pressure he was put under by her continued staring. Dogs will do this if they think there is not too much danger of attack, but feel uncomfortable and pressured and wish to turn down the heat.

DID YOU KNOW?

❑ Dogs have several strategies for calming potential aggressors. These include:

- yawning
- averting their eyes
- lip-licking
- turning their heads
- sniffing something on the floor
- play-bowing
- sitting down
- sitting with their back to you
- walking away very slowly
- approaching another individual in a wide arc rather than directly as this may be considered less confrontational.

Avoiding a fight

When threatened, dogs can use aggression to defend themselves, but this is usually a last resort when all else has failed. Before they choose this course of action, they have to weigh up the chances of success. If the use of aggression fails to work, their rival does not back down and they lose the fight, they risk being killed or injured.

Consequently, most dogs will try a whole range of other tactics before resorting to violence. These vary, depending on the dog's experience, from elaborate body postures to strategies for staying out of trouble such as simply ignoring the problem, walking away or concentrating on other things instead. Only if these approaches fail, the threat appears too suddenly, or they learn that these strategies don't work, will they exercise aggression.

Don't bite me

The boxer isn't sure about the intentions of the other dog as she is not very experienced at reading body language. She has turned sideways on until she and the other dog form a T-shape. This means that her rear end is not vulnerable and they are not head to head. She has turned her head away to reduce further the risk of conflict.

Must cool down

Having averted a possible fight, and unsure of what to do next, drinking becomes a 'safe' option. This turns off the interaction with the other dog, as does sniffing a blade of grass or any other harmless activity. The hackles along her back and neck are still slightly raised and will continue to signal her alarm until she calms down.

Better get out of here

The confident sandy-coloured dog signals his readiness to have an encounter by raising his tail and moving forward. Not wishing to get into trouble, the lurcher moves away slowly. Moving too quickly may encourage a chase, so he lowers his tail, pulls back his ears as if frightened and walks off slowly. In this position, his rear end is vulnerable, so he turns his head so that he is able to keep a close eye on the other dog's movements.

The excessive arching of his tail over his back and the raised hackles on his shoulder indicate that the sandy-coloured dog is not quite as confident as he would like to appear.

DID YOU KNOW?

- How well dogs interact with each other will depend on how many good encounters they had with different dogs during their puppyhood.
- Well-socialized dogs easily diffuse an aggressive situation and rarely get into fights.
- Poorly socialized dogs do not read the subtle signals of others and find it difficult to send proper signals themselves, so often get into trouble.

Hope he doesn't follow

This dog is worried by a strong, powerful dog behind him. He moves away slowly, hoping not to trigger an attack. He is old and stiff and cannot turn his head very far round to keep track of the problem, so he swivels his eyes as much as possible instead so that the whites of them can be seen against his dark fur.

Body language of fear

Dogs that are frightened show it very obviously and, if you know what to look for, you can prevent them from becoming even more worried and biting in self-defence. Some dogs mask their fear in a display of confidence and bravado but, underneath, they are as worried as dogs that run away. Confusingly, some dogs will give an array of different signals as they pass through a range of emotions. Watching for the different signals from tails, ears and bodies can help to unravel these signals and give you a better idea of what the dog is thinking.

Oh-oh!

This dog is worried about something in front of her and is pulling back to get away. Her tail is tucked right under and her ears are held well back so they would be out of the way if she were attacked. Her eyes are fixed on whatever is scaring her in case she needs to get away more quickly and the whites of her eyes are showing as her eyes open wide to gather more information. Her heart will be racing and her body will be preparing itself for flight or fight.

I'm worried

Being asked to lie down in a stressful situation causes this dog to worry. Being placed in a vulnerable position, which makes it more difficult for him to run away, can add to any other concerns. His ears are back, eyes open wide and he pants rapidly with stress.

DID YOU KNOW?

❏ You can learn a lot about what your dog is feeling from his body language:

- ears pulled back: he is frightened or submissive
- ears forward: he is confident or interested
- eyes, whites showing and large pupils: he is frightened
- mouth wide and panting quickly: he is frightened
- tail lowered: he is frightened or submissive
- tail raised: he is confident
- tail wagging: he is excited.

Don't come closer

This is the face of fear and defensive aggression. The ears are back and the mouth is wide with worry. However, the lips are drawn slightly up to expose the teeth, the head is up ready to bite and the eyes are fixed on the antagonist so that further aggressive action can be taken if necessary. This face is accompanied by a series of explosive alarm barks designed to make the aggressor move away so that a dangerous fight does not ensue.

Oh dear

Finding a safe place is essential if you are scared. This dog has moved to the best position in this area but has nowhere to hide or feel really safe. He stands waiting miserably for better options to become available, all the time keeping eyes and ears alert for anything too scary that he may need to run away from.

Strategies for safety

Staying safe is a top priority in the wild where there is no one to rescue you if you are injured. If your dog is threatened he can choose from the four strategies of fight, flight, freeze and appease to help him deal with the problem he has encountered. Dogs can move rapidly between the four different states depending on how successful the one they have chosen is proving and how great the threat they are facing seems to be.

If I keep still, I'll be all right

Some dogs will freeze and hope that the potential attacker will go away and leave them alone. Usually dogs that do this will watch carefully and begin to move away or become aggressive if the threat gets too close. This dog is hemmed in by the others and has no choice but to hope that things don't turn nasty. She turns her head away to show her concern.

I'll just stay here

This spaniel spent the first four years of her life living in a shed, so she is scared of new circumstances and people. She hasn't enough confidence to use aggression, doesn't know where to run to for safety and so she chooses to remain motionless and hope everyone will stay away from her. If they come too close and this option seems unsuccessful, she will run away to maintain a safe distance.

Be silly too?

The terrier has maintained a stationary erect posture with raised tail and full stare as a way of preventing any further contact. This is quite threatening for the other dog, which tries an appeasement gesture in the hope that she can jolly the terrier out of her static state. She play-bows briefly so that she is not in a vulnerable position for too long. Her face is full of concern as shown by her pulled-back ears, wide mouth and flicking tongue. She keeps her eyes fixed on the other dog in case she needs to change her strategy quickly.

DID YOU KNOW?

- Dogs may feel forced to choose the 'fight' option in circumstances where they feel cornered. You should watch your dog carefully for any signs of unease and take him away from a situation that is causing him concern.

I'm just a silly puppy

This puppy is trying the appeasement strategy, but the signals are tinged with fear. He has lowered his body and is wagging his lowered tail slowly from side to side to signal appeasement. However, his shoulders are raised and he keeps his eyes on the person coming towards him in case he needs to change his strategy quickly.

Guarding territory

If dogs have sufficient confidence, chasing away a threat to themselves or their pack may be a better option than freezing or running away. Usually this is done at boundaries of the territory, such as at the garden gate, front door or over the fence, as it is at these places that the dog has most chance of success. If he encounters a stranger who has been bold enough to come onto the territory uninvited, it is likely that, in a similar way to humans, he will have less confidence in his ability to deal with the situation.

Stay away

This Doberman feels confident about keeping strangers away from his pen, and leans forward and barks threateningly. If he had a tail, it would be held confidently upright. His mouth is small and his ears forward. Dogs that show aggressive guarding behaviour may appear to be in control, and indeed, may be in control of a situation, but usually their actions are based on fear. A telltale sign is that the hackles on his neck are beginning to rise to make him appear bigger than he really is. The reason behind this behaviour is a mistrust of strangers, as he was not properly socialized with people from an early age. If he was truly confident of others, he would have no need to put on such a good display of aggression to keep everyone away.

DID YOU KNOW?

❑ Dogs of the guarding breeds, such as Rottweilers and Dobermans, have been bred to show less fear than other breeds, making it harder to tell what they are thinking. They have also been bred to have more confidence, making it more likely that they will choose the fight option if they feel they are in danger.

Get away from here

The postman is the traditional target of aggression from dogs. This is because he comes every day at a set time, does something strange that no one else does, like pushing letters through the hole in the door, and then, when barked at, runs away. Since the dog is rewarded by, as he sees it, the postman retreating, he becomes more confident about seeing him off and is likely to be more aggressive than usual if the door is left open. This dog has risen to the challenge of seeing off the intruder at the door, but her confidence is not high, as may be seen from her lowered tail.

Keep out!

Rottweilers have been bred specifically to be guard dogs and to have enough confidence to look after themselves and their territory. For a dog to be aggressive to people coming onto its property, it must see them as a threat. For this reason, an in-built suspicion of strangers is useful in a guard dog, especially if this is accentuated by limited contact with people during puppyhood. This dog looks as though he means business with his upright stance and his strong eye contact. He has come right to the end of the rope that tethers him and so must have the confidence to deal with the intruder. The dribble in the corner of his mouth indicates that he is in an agitated state, and so it would not be wise to approach him at this time.

Decisions for safety

If a dog or his territory is threatened, he needs to base his decision on what action to take on his ability to defend himself and protect his resources. He needs to weigh up the chances of winning against the risk of injury to himself. During dangerous encounters, continuous assessment of the risks involved is necessary so that the appropriate action can be taken as and when required. This strategy helps to keep the dog as safe as possible while at the same time maximizing the chances of success.

Don't come closer

Seeing a threat to his territory, this dog puts on a brave display. He has come to the gate and is barking. However, his ear and tail carriage betray his true feelings of inadequacy and tell us that he is not completely committed to getting rid of us. His ears are back, his tail is down and his weight is mostly on his hind legs so that he is ready to run if necessary. His lips are held down, covering his teeth so as not to antagonize us further. His warning bark is probably designed to bring reinforcements in the form of other members of his pack to help him out, rather than to keep us away.

Time to retreat

Having decided that he does not have the ability to hold his ground, he retreats to a safe distance. He moves away quickly so that we don't have time to catch up with him. If the threat was greater or approaching more quickly, or there was not a gate in between us, he would have moved even faster, keeping a lookout over his shoulder so that he could review his position rapidly and change his strategy if necessary.

I feel safer here

From a safe distance, he resumes his defence of the property. He now has more room to manoeuvre, but having been forced to withdraw once, his confidence is very low. He ceases to bark but keeps a watch on our movements in case we encroach further onto his territory. Dogs like this, that have little confidence in their ability to defend themselves or their territory, rely heavily on their pack leaders to keep them safe and can feel very vulnerable if left alone.

There is little danger that dogs like this one will bite someone, but it is better to try to ensure that dogs are well socialized as puppies so that they have no need to fear humans. A combination of good socialization and a happy, safe environment usually produces a dog that is friendly towards strangers.

DID YOU KNOW?

❑ Dogs of all breeds are capable of behaving aggressively if they feel sufficiently threatened.

❑ How threatened a dog feels will depend on previous experiences in similar situations and on the nature of his encounters with humans and other animals, particularly those that occurred during puppyhood.

❑ The amount of aggression a dog shows will depend upon:

- how big the threat is
- how much natural confidence it inherited from its parents and
- how successful it has been during previous encounters throughout its life.

Dogs and people

Dogs do not instinctively understand our body language and have to learn about us from an early age if they are to fit in with us easily. Something as simple as eye contact, which humans use in a friendly way, can send poorly socialized dogs running for cover if they are not used to it. Most humans do not know enough about how dogs see the world and misunderstandings between man and dog arise frequently. Sadly, the dog is often blamed for these despite humans being the more intelligent species. Realizing that dogs are not actually little humans in furry skins, and finding out how to interact with them successfully, leads to a much happier relationship between dogs and people.

Are you friendly?

This dog is well socialized with people and takes this quite threatening approach in his stride. Leaning forward and looking intently at the dog in this way would be enough to overwhelm many dogs. However, this dog seems unafraid, although he is leaning back a little so that his front feet are sloping rather than upright. These two have just been playing a game so the dog has no reason to feel worried by this person. If this was to continue for too long, however, the dog may begin to feel more uncomfortable.

Safe or scary?

These two have just met and are not yet friends. The dog has been well socialized with people and has learnt that eye contact can be friendly and unthreatening. So she returns the gaze and watches to see what the person will do next. She is a little worried, as seen by her tail that is tucked underneath her, her pulled-back ears and her wide, open mouth. She is panting a little through stress and is not quite sure what to do next.

Are you okay?

As she is used to people, this dog takes this rather awkward human greeting well. Bending over so that face and eyes are on the same level and extending the hands in this way would be quite threatening to a less confident dog. This dog is not overjoyed to be greeted in this way, but is interested in getting to know this person more, as may be seen by her upright ears and her nose which is sniffing to find out more about him. Her tail is held in a neutral position indicating that she is not worried, excited, happy or anxious.

DID YOU KNOW?

- Dogs predominantly use their nose and mouth to find out about their world whereas humans use their eyes and hands. Keeping eye and hand contact to a minimum when greeting dogs can reduce their fear and help us make friends with them more quickly.

I'm not sure

This person continues to lean over while trying to reach out and stroke her. She is now getting a little concerned about him, as may be seen by the ears that are flattening against her head and by the movement of her front feet away from him. If he were to crouch down, turn sideways slightly and look away, she would probably feel more comfortable and move closer.

Don't stare

Dogs threaten each other by staring and they learn quickly to take avoiding action if this happens rather than risk the resulting aggression that would otherwise accompany it. Humans will gaze lovingly at their pet and consequently dogs need to learn that staring from humans is okay. Dogs rarely learn this properly, however, and will display a whole range of signs that they are uneasy when stared at, most of which go completely unrecognized and unnoticed by their owners.

I'm worried

The prolonged stare is worrying this boxer. She has turned away and sat down but she is still not comfortable with the social pressure being exerted. Her mouth is wide and she is panting a little with the stress. Her ears are pulled back and she looks straight ahead so that she doesn't have to engage in any sort of interaction. The person has leaned forward so that she is closer and their eyes are level and this has added to the dog's feeling of discomfort.

DID YOU KNOW?

- ❑ Compared to adults, children have proportionally larger eyes, they are more likely to stare, and their eyes are often on a level with dogs' eyes. Consequently, they can appear more frightening to poorly socialized dogs.
- ❑ A dog's vision is not so detailed as ours, and they recognize different objects by smell and shape rather than by detail and texture.
- ❑ Dogs can see in colour, although not as well as humans, and they can see better in low light levels.

You can't see me

This dog is enjoying being with a person she knows quite well. She has leaned her body against her and is sweeping her tail from side to side in a big, wide greeting gesture. Dogs that are not too confident about people often present their bottoms for stroking rather than risk their front end. Having done so, she would like to have more contact and she turns her head looking for more fuss. As she does so, she catches the person's eyes which are staring at her in a happy human way. This is too much for her and, rather than turn her head away and lose the contact, she closes her eyes to break the intensity of the stare.

Stare at me, would you?

These two dogs are rivals and both have enough confidence to stand their ground. Neither really wants a fight but neither will back down so a standoff ensues. Holding eye contact becomes essential as each tries to stare the other down. The one to break off the eye contact will be the loser and both will know next time they encounter each other which one lost the previous contest.

Kind hands

Dogs often use their mouths to hold and touch things whereas we use our hands. Our pet dogs need to get used to this and learn to appreciate being touched. Most dogs learn to enjoy being stroked and fussed by our hands and are happy to be touched by us. This is particularly true if dogs have grown up with gentle, kind humans who did not hit or push them around with their hands when they were puppies. Dogs that have learnt to trust humans in this way can be groomed easily and are not afraid of the hands of strangers coming towards them.

I like you

This friendly collie allows herself to be touched and is accepting the contact. From her point of view, this is a good place to touch as the hand doesn't cover any sense organs and is low down so it is not likely to hit or grab. She is well socialized with people and is happy to hold eye contact. She enjoys physical contact and is about to move closer.

It's okay to touch there

The greyhound is not so sure about people as he was brought up in a racing yard with limited contact with humans. He tolerates this most gentle of touches, particularly since this person has turned sideways and is not looking at him, but he is not comfortable, as may be seen by his pulled-back ears and his tense body. His head is held straight to avoid any chance of a face-to-face encounter and he pants rapidly with the stress of the experience.

Come here!

The puppy paws at the other dog as they play. The black dog looks surprised and moves away as she is not used to this sort of play. The puppy may have been trying to place two paws on her back and stand up, a common position during play, but one that seems to be viewed by others as quite rude and competitive. Dogs only use their paws during fighting, mating and playing. The rest of the time paws are used for running on so it must seem strange to them that humans like to use their hands so much.

DID YOU KNOW?

- ❏ More people are bitten by dogs on the hands than on any other part of the body.
- ❏ Children use their hands to find out about their world whereas puppies use their mouths for the same purpose.

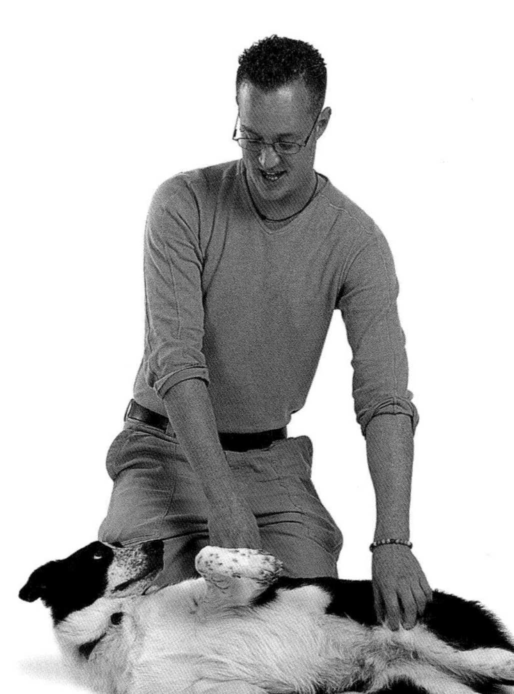

A bit slower please

This collie would prefer to be stroked on her chest which is a 'safe' zone, and has raised her front paw to indicate this. The person persists in stroking her back leg which is too close to her belly and other sensitive areas to be comfortable. Since she cannot relax until he moves his hand, she turns her head to look at him to check whether his intentions are safe or dangerous. Being very trusting of humans, she continues to lie still while she monitors the situation carefully and waits for him to be better mannered with his touches.

Don't touch

Dogs often have to surrender control of what is happening to them to the person who is holding their lead. Imagine how it would feel if a perfect stranger approached and, after talking in a different language to the person you were with, began to touch you. Dogs have to learn to put up with this and, to their credit, many even learn to enjoy it. However, we can make things easier for them if we learn where the sensitive areas are. We can then stay away from these areas when touching an unfamiliar dog and desensitize our own dogs to being touched there.

That's okay

The back and chest are 'safe' areas and dogs rapidly become used to being touched here. This dog is comfortable with this type of touching and relaxes, focusing her interest elsewhere. She has had a kind owner but is not used to being touched by strangers. She tolerates this type of touching well and even seems to draw some strength from being close to someone she can get to know.

Don't like that

While she is sitting down, she is touched underneath the chest in the belly region. This is not a normal approach and she becomes concerned. Her expression changes, she becomes tense and her ears are pulled back. She has little dots of fawn on her eyebrows and under her ears, making her expressions very easy to read. She is being touched in a sensitive area and although the touch is very gentle, she is disturbed by it and would rather not be touched there.

Or that

Between the hind legs is another sensitive area where she would rather not be touched. She tries to sit down so that this can't be done and the person has to hold her collar to prevent her doing so. She is tense and has moved her weight onto her hind legs to make it more difficult. This is a place where dogs would not touch each other and she makes it clear that there is no need for a person to do so either.

A bit better

This dog is used to being handled, but a hug from a total stranger is a bit much. Since it is done very slowly and the person doesn't lean over her, she just about tolerates it, but her tail is down and her ears are slightly back. She is spoken to reassuringly, but she would rather the person returned to stroking her back and chest, areas about which she feels much more comfortable.

Scary hands

Some dogs will not have had enough pleasant experiences with human hands when they were puppies and, worse still, some will have learnt that hands are often used to smack or cause discomfort. Dog bites are often directed towards hands for this reason. Being careful with our hands and moving them slowly can help dogs learn that our hands are safe and bring food and other rewards instead of dangers.

I can't see

We usually stroke a dog's head as it is often the bit that is easiest to reach. As we do so, we often cover up the sense organs that enable the dog to monitor his environment. This includes covering the eyes, touching the delicate whiskers around the muzzle and vibrissae around the face and covering the ears. This temporarily blocks off their view of the world and can be very worrying, especially for nervous dogs. Patting them on the head is even worse as it jars and shakes their vision.

I can't hear

Stroking and playing with their ears can temporarily stop them from hearing properly. This dog is confident and relaxed with people and does not mind, but a dog that is worried about its environment may not be able to cope so well. It is best to reserve head-stroking for dogs that know you well. With dogs that are unfamiliar, gently touch their chest and stay well away from all the organs that allow them to take in information about their world.

Are you going to attack me?

This is not a good way to greet an unfamiliar dog, but many people approach dogs like this. This dog has kind owners, but his early life has made him shy with strangers. Consequently, this exuberant greeting worries him and he tries to shrink away. His ears are back, his eyes wide open, his tail is tucked between his legs and he looks as though he is deciding whether or not he should move away.

Ooh, you look scary

From your dog's point of view, human hands coming towards his head can look quite frightening. In addition, this person has leant forward and is making eye contact and has spoken to the dog. The dog is not sure of his intentions and so turns his head away to try to diffuse the situation and end the encounter.

DID YOU KNOW?

- Puppies need to learn that human hands come to stroke and give treats rather than punish. If all dogs learned this early on in life, fewer people would be bitten by dogs as they try to defend themselves.

Ticklish spot

Most dogs enjoy being tickled and rubbed in certain places. These may be places they cannot get to easily themselves, especially if the dog is old or stiff, or they may be just favourite spots where they enjoy being scratched or stroked. Regular sessions with grooming, stroking and scratching of ticklish places help to establish a trust of hands and also to strengthen the bond of companionship between dog and owner.

Just there is perfect

Chest areas and areas around the collar are often favourite scratching places. They are hard for your dog to scratch as the collar gets in the way and this area is often irritated by the movement of the collar and its tags against the neck. Scratching here can send your dog into apparent ecstasy, with an accompanying jerking of a hind leg as he tries to help out in reaching the exact spot that will provide him with relief.

Up a bit please

Behind the ears is another favourite spot that is hard to get to unless the dog is young and agile. This dog has turned his head to one side to get into a better position and may prefer it if he were scratched a bit higher. Dogs that enjoy this often close their eyes in apparent pleasure and seem to become oblivious to the rest of the world.

Under here please

This dog has lifted his front paw to encourage his owner to rub his chest – a favourite place for dogs to be stroked. This dog isn't as relaxed he should be for this type of stroking, as may be seen by his slightly raised head and his focus on his owner. This could be because the owner isn't actually relaxed either and the dog is poised ready to spring up to play if released.

DID YOU KNOW?

❑ Stroking dogs has been proven to have a beneficial effect on the blood pressure of the human doing the stroking. So as well as being pleasurable for your dog, it is good for you too.

That's nice

Gentle massaging is sometimes preferable to scratching and this dog is enjoying his owner's attentions. He has tilted his head to one side, his face and eyes are relaxed and his mouth is pulled up over one lip giving him an odd expression. His body is relaxed, his tail is not tucked in and there is no sign of tension. Massaging your dog in this way could be beneficial not only for him but also for you as it is difficult to produce this degree of contentment without being relaxed yourself.

Hand signals

One way to make human hands more acceptable is to make sure they contain tasty treats and toys to play with. Not only does this help dogs to view hands in a positive light, but it also enables us to develop hand signals which aid communication. Since dogs learn body language easily, it is quite simple to teach them signals for sitting, waiting or coming to us once they have learnt to focus on our hands. Later, we can add words to these actions until, eventually, we can phase out the actions and our dogs will respond instantly and accurately to the spoken words alone.

Where is it?

This sheepdog is deaf and the only way to communicate with her is by sight. Teaching her to follow hands that are holding a titbit is the first step. The titbit is held in between the fingers so that the hand can be held flat. As she moves to take the titbit, the hand is slowly drawn away. Gradually she will learn to follow an outstretched flattened hand even when there is no titbit attached, and this can be a useful technique for moving her to different locations.

I'm being good

Teaching her to sit is easy once she has learnt to watch hands for titbits. Holding the treat over her head causes her to hold her head back so that she can see it. After a while, this becomes uncomfortable and she sits down. The titbit is given immediately and, after a few sessions, she realizes that sitting down when someone holds out their hand above her causes the titbit to be delivered. Eventually, the hand signal alone becomes the cue to sit, and the rewards can then be given randomly to reinforce the action.

Here I come

Some dogs would rather work for a game with a toy than for food. This dog is excited by movement and twists and turns to catch up with the ball. Dogs that like activity are easy to teach if you want them to walk, run or jump but not so easy if you want them to stay still.

DID YOU KNOW?

❑ Dogs can be rewarded by many things, although it is not possible to use all of them during training, and different dogs will appreciate different rewards. Rewards that can be used include food, games, running and your approval.

Give it to me

Playing with squeaky toys is this dog's favourite game and he is so focused on the toy that it is possible to position him exactly where he is wanted by holding it in the right position. The person waits for him to sit before throwing it so that he learns to control his excitement. The reward of the game will ensure that he is likely to go back into that position again easily next time. By concealing a smaller toy in her hand, it would be easy for his owner to teach him hand signals as he is a clever dog and learns quickly.

I'm waiting

This dog has learnt to sit if he wants the toy to be thrown. Over several sessions he has learnt to wait for longer and longer, and now sits patiently in the certain knowledge that he will get an exciting chase game eventually.

Human emotions?

Do dogs feel jealousy, anger, affection or other human emotions? Since they cannot talk, we are not able to ask them, and all we can do is make an assessment based on their reactions and body language. If you take enough time and observe dogs closely, they do seem to express similar emotions to ours in similar situations. We may never know for certain, but until we do, we should, at least, take into account that they may experience similar feelings to those we experience ourselves.

Can I join in?

Sometimes, owners attribute the emotion of jealousy to a dog when he interrupts an intimate moment. In fact, he may just be seizing the opportunity to get some friendly attention. This Basset Hound loves affection from her owners and seizes the moment while they are sitting down and in a friendly mood to get some for herself. When she climbs on top of them, she is difficult to ignore!

Stay away from her

This dog has had some bad experiences with men in the past and may be genuinely worried about his precious owner being so close to someone that may be dangerous. By getting in between, and pressing himself backwards so that he can see her, he may be hoping to help her out if she gets into difficulties. Alternatively, he may just be trying to get some attention for himself.

DID YOU KNOW?

- Although dogs can appear to have a supernatural ability or extrasensory perception, their ability to detect things we cannot hear, see or smell can usually be explained by their amazing 'super' senses, which help them view the world in a very different way to the way we do.

Soon be home

Some dogs seem to know when their owners are returning and will begin waiting by the door or window as they turn for home. Experiments have proved that this is more than coincidence and that these dogs are not responding to any known physical signs or signals. Could they be picking up their owners' thoughts in some way? There may be much more to the way dogs see the world than we could ever imagine.

I'm enjoying this

A dog's love of affection from his owners is what makes them special to us. Love and loyalty are high on the list of characteristics owners require in a dog. This has to be a two-way process. Although in a vulnerable position, this dog is totally relaxed because he trusts his owner completely. By understanding more about how dogs view the world, it should be possible for more owners to build a loving and trusting relationship with their dog.

Index

Acknowledgements

I would like to thank all the people who have taught me so much about animal behaviour, and especially about body language over the years, including John Rogerson, Ian Dunbar, Roger Abrantes, Michael Fox and Turrid Ruggass. Thanks are also due to Ryan Neile, a behaviourist with great promise for the future, for reading the proofs, making useful comments and for his enthusiasm for the project.

I am grateful also to Julie Stone and Ryan Neile for so carefully handling and choosing the dogs for the photographs, and to Steve Gorton for taking such beautiful pictures, often when only one chance at a shot was possible. I am grateful to the owners who loaned their lovely dogs and to The Blue Cross who allowed us to photograph some of the many dogs in their care awaiting homes.

I would also like to thank the people at Hamlyn who made the book possible and especially to Sharon Ashman, Julian Brown and Leigh Jones for their help and encouragement.

And finally, I would like to mention Beau, the last of my pack of three dogs and a very old man at 14 years. Thank you for all you have taught me, for sleeping contentedly in your bed while I wrote this book, and for sharing your long life with me.

Gwen Bailey

Executive editor Trevor Davies
Editor Sharon Ashman
Executive art editor Leigh Jones
Designer Louise Griffiths
Picture researcher Zoë Holterman
Production controller Edward Carter
Special photography Steve Gorton

Photographic Acknowledgements

Blue Cross/Rosie Hyde 19 top right, 69 top right, 72 bottom right
Corbis UK Ltd/David A. Northcott 34 top/Marcello Calandrini 24 left /Tom Brakefield 8
David Key 22 top right, 28 top right
Gwen Bailey 35 top left, 50 bottom left, 53 top right, 64
Warren Photographic/Jane Burton 65 top, 65 bottom
All other photographs **Octopus Publishing Group Limited**/Steve Gorton